CALIFORNIA GOVERNMENT SERIES

A CONSTITUTION

for

CALIFORNIA

CALIFORNIA GOVERNMENT SERIES

A
CONSTITUTION
for
CALIFORNIA

Bennett Jacobstein

Toucan Valley Publications, Inc.

Available from:
Toucan Valley Publications, Inc.
PO Box 15520
Fremont CA 94539-2620

Phone: (800) 236-7946
Fax: (888) 391-6943
E-mail: query@toucanvalley.com

Web site: **www.toucanvalley.com**

Manufactured in the United States of America
First Edition

Contents

1

What is a constitution?

A constitution contains the basic ideas and principles on which the government of an organization is based. A constitution could be for a group, such as the American Medical Association, or for a government, such as a country or a state.

The constitution of a country or state usually contains the basic rights that its citizens have, as well as the way the government is organized and what tasks each branch of government performs. It also may determine who is a citizen and who has the right to vote. Many constitutions also put limits on the power of the government.

Most of the laws of a country or state are not in the constitution, but in separate books of laws. However, no laws can be passed that violate (go against) what is written in its constitution.

A constitution also includes ways that it can be amended (changed) at future dates. This is necessary because new issues may come along, or the views of the people may change over time.

The idea for a constitution was originated by Aristotle. He was an ancient Greek philosopher who lived over 2,000 years ago. Constitutions for governments, however, did not become popular until the 18th century.

2

California needed a constitution in a hurry

In 1822, California became part of Mexico, which had just achieved its independence from Spain. Twenty-four years later, in 1846, American settlers led by Ezekiel Merritt, with the backing of U.S. Army Captain John Frémont, revolted against the Mexican government. The uprising was known as the *Bear Flag Revolt* because of a grizzly bear that was drawn with blackberry juice on the settler's flag. Soon naval forces led by Commodore Sloat and army troops led by General Stephen Kearny arrived in California, sent by the U.S. government to take over California. From 1846 to 1848, United States and Mexico were involved in what became known as the *Mexican War*.

The war ended on February 2, 1848, with the signing of the *Treaty of Guadalupe Hidalgo*. (The treaty was named for the village in Mexico where the negotiations took place). As a result of the treaty, Mexico gave to the United States the land that makes up present-day California, as well as Nevada, Utah, and parts of Arizona, New Mexico, Colorado, and Wyoming. This area was known as the *Mexican Cession*.

The Mexican Cession

During the Mexican War, California was under military rule and led by military governors. Once the war ended, however, the people wanted to have a regular elected government. But nobody knew what kind of government there should be. Although California was now part of the United States, it was neither a state nor a territory.

Richard Mason, who was then the military governor, asked the U.S. Congress to organize a territorial government in California. But the members of Congress argued amongst themselves, and were divided as to whether the California Territory should be a *slave-territory* or a *free-territory*. A *slave-territory* means that slavery (which was allowed at the time in the southern states) would be allowed in California, and a *free-territory* means that slavery would **not** be allowed. Congress could not reach an agreement, and as a result did nothing to establish a government in California.

California now had no official government or laws. Sometimes the former Mexican laws were used, sometimes local *alcaldes* (mayors) made up their own laws, and sometimes no laws were used at all. As a result there was a great deal of confusion and the California people were becoming very restless.

And then the situation became even worse, as many people from all lands flooded into California as part of the great gold rush. Arguments arose over land and gold mine claims, and the need for laws and government was becoming desperate. Governor Mason was frustrated by the situation and requested to return to Missouri. He was replaced briefly by General Persifor Smith, who was followed by General Bennett Riley.

General Riley realized by this time that Congress would not help the people of California and that they needed to take action on their own. Zachary Taylor, the President of the United States, gave General Riley a suggestion. He recommended that California write its own constitution, and then petition (ask) the Congress to admit California as a state (without it first becoming a territory).

General Riley took the President's advice, and this is why California needed a constitution in a hurry.

3

The constitutional convention of 1849

On June 3, 1849, General Riley issued a proclamation (an announcement) ordering a constitutional convention. A constitutional convention means that selected individuals will gather together for the purpose of writing a new constitution. The individuals, known as delegates, would be chosen by an election to be held on August 1, 1849.

The delegates would be elected from different districts (areas) of California. Thirty-seven delegates would be elected from the districts as follows:

San Diego District...2 delegates
Los Angeles District.......................................4 delegates
Santa Barbara District....................................2 delegates
San Luis Obispo District.................................2 delegates
Monterey District...5 delegates
San Jose District..5 delegates
San Francisco District....................................5 delegates
Sonoma District...4 delegates
Sacramento District..4 delegates
San Joaquin District.......................................4 delegates

If any district wanted to send additional delegates, they could go to the convention, and the elected members of the convention would then vote on whether or not to allow the additional delegates to attend. As it turned out, thirteen additional people showed up, and they were all allowed to join the convention. Also, Santa Barbara and Sonoma each sent one fewer delegate than they were allocated. This made for a total of 48 (37 + 13 - 2) delegates who were given the task of writing California's first constitution. The actual delegates attending the convention by district were as follows:

San Diego District...2 delegates
Los Angeles District.......................................5 delegates
Santa Barbara District....................................1 delegate
San Luis Obispo District.................................2 delegates

Monterey District ....6 delegates
San Jose District...7 delegates
San Francisco District ....8 delegates
Sonoma District...3 delegates
Sacramento District ....8 delegates
San Joaquin District ....6 delegates

The 48 delegates (all of them men) were natives of 16 different states and five foreign countries (Switzerland, France, Scotland, Ireland, and Spain). Many of the delegates had only been in California a short time. The most common occupations represented were lawyers, farmers, and merchants. The group was quite young, with 27 delegates under the age of 35, and only three delegates over the age of 50. Seven of the delegates were Hispano-Californians (natives of California of Mexican origin) who did not speak English. William Hartnell, a bi-lingual resident of Monterey, was appointed to be the interpreter of the convention.

The convention was held at Colton Hall, located in the town of Monterey. It was scheduled to start on September 1, 1849, but some of the delegates had not arrived by that date. Roads were not very good and travel was very difficult. Delegates from southern California came by ship and were delayed by fog. By September 3, the delegates had arrived in Monterey and the convention began.

Colton Hall, Monterey

Dr. Robert Semple, a dentist from Benicia, was elected president of the convention. Rev. S. H. Willey and Padre Ramirez, local clergymen, were appointed chaplains of the convention and each day the convention began with a prayer. The convention started with the reading of a message from General Riley:

> "You have important work before you: the beginning of a state. The future of the state depends upon you. Your materials are good. Let it never be said that you, the builders, lacked skill in putting them together."

At the time of the convention the United States consisted of 30 states. Each of those states had a state constitution. Those constitutions, as well as the U.S. Constitution, were used as models for the new California constitution. The constitutions of Iowa and New York were of particular help as models.

A major decision the delegates needed to make was how much power to give to the legislators (the people who would be elected to make the laws after California became a state). Some state constitutions included very few specific laws because their writers believed the legislators would always represent the people and act in their best interest. Other state constitutions included many specific laws because their writers were afraid future legislators might not always act in the people's best interest. The delegates to the California convention took a middle ground and included some specific laws, but also granted a great deal of power to the future legislators.

The first order of business was to establish a *Declaration of Rights*. These were important rights for the citizens similar to the *Bill of Rights* in the U.S. Constitution. Some of the rights included freedom of religion, freedom of speech, and the right to a jury trial. The delegates wanted to make sure that future legislators could never take these rights away.

The delegates established three branches of government similar to all the other states and to the Federal government. This system is known as the *separation of powers*, and contains the legislative branch (represented by the Senate and Assembly), the executive branch (represented by the governor), and the judicial branch (represented by the Supreme Court). This system prevents any single branch of government from becoming too powerful.

Two issues of controversy were slavery and the right of Indians to vote. Although the delegates voted to prohibit slavery, not all the opposition was due to the belief that slavery was morally wrong. Many delegates believed that allowing slavery would cost jobs and give control of the gold mines to the wealthy. After heated debate about the right of Indians to vote, the delegates decided not to decide the issue, but instead to leave it to the first legislators.

The last major issue to be decided was the state boundary. Some delegates wanted the boundary of California to include the entire Mexican Cession, which included present-day California as well as Nevada, Utah, and parts of Arizona, New Mexico, Colorado and Wyoming. Other delegates wanted the boundary to include only what is now present-day California. The only settlement in the Mexican Cession area outside of present-day California at the time was the Mormon settlement in Utah. The delegates decided on the smaller boundary for several reasons. Some felt the larger area would be too hard to govern. Others felt it would be unfair to include the Mormon settlement because no one from that settlement was invited to the convention. Finally, John Sutter, a delegate from Sacramento who had owned the land where gold was first discovered, said that the larger area "was a great desert . . . of no value whatever."

After six weeks of work, on October 13, 1849, the delegates completed their task and the constitution was signed. The ships in Monterey harbor unfurled their flags and a 31-gun salute was fired, symbolizing California's future as America's 31st state. A great ball was held that night in Colton Hall, and the delegates and their guests celebrated well into the night.

The final step for California's constitution was approval by the voters. An election was held on November 13, 1849, and the constitution was approved by a vote of 12,061 to 811. Ten months later, on September 9, 1850, California was admitted to the Union as the 31st state.

4

The people who wrote the constitution

Forty-eight men wrote the California Constitution. Some of them, such as John Sutter or Mariano Vallejo, played other roles in California's history; others are remembered mainly for their signatures on this document.

Joseph Aram, representing the District of San Jose, was a native of New York who came from Illinois in 1846. He was a farmer, partner in the trading firm of Aram & Belcher, and served in the first State Legislature.

Charles T. Botts, representing the District of Monterey, was a native of Virginia who came to California by ship on the *Matilda* in 1848. He was a lawyer with a major San Francisco law firm from 1850-58, and then moved to Sacramento where he published the *Standard*. He served as the State Printer and as a district judge before retiring to Oakland.

Elam Brown, representing the District of San Jose, was a native of New York who immigrated from Missouri in 1846, serving as the captain of his party. In 1847 he bought the Acalanes Rancho in Contra Costa and lived there for many years. He was a member of the first State Legislature.

José Antonio Carillo, representing the District of Los Angeles, was a native of California born in San Francisco. He was a teacher and then became *alcalde* (mayor) of Los Angeles in 1827. During the Mexican War, he led the Mexican troops in the battle to control Los Angeles. Although they won that battle, soon afterwards they lost the war and he was a signer of the Cahuenga Treaty, which ended the war between Mexican and American forces in California.

José María Covarrubias, representing the District of San Luis Obispo, was a native of France and a naturalized citizen of Mexico. He came to California in 1834 to work as a teacher, and later became personal secretary to Governor Pico. In 1843 he was granted the Castac Rancho. He was a member of the first State Legislature and later served as a county judge in Santa Barbara.

Elisha O. Crosby, representing the District of Sacramento, was a native of New York who came to California in 1848. As a respected lawyer, he helped create the State court system. He was the founder of the Yuba County community of Vernon.

Pablo De La Guerra, representing the District of Santa Barbara, was a native of California. He was an *alcalde* (mayor) of Santa Barbara and in 1844 was granted the Nicasio Rancho. During the Mexican War he was imprisoned for a brief time. Later he served as a State senator, acting lieutenant governor, U.S. marshall, and district judge.

Miguel De Pedrorena, representing the District of San Diego, was a native of Spain who came to California in 1837. His family was very powerful in Spain and his brother held a high official position. In 1846, he was granted the San Jacinto Nuevo Rancho. He was an American supporter during the Mexican War and served as an aide to Commodore Stockton.

Lewis Dent, representing the District of Monterey, was a native of Missouri who came to California in 1847. He was a lawyer in the firm of Dent and Martin. He served briefly as a circuit judge in California before leaving to become a lawyer and politician in Mississippi, Missouri, and Washington.

Kimball H. Dimmick, representing the District of San Jose, was a native of Connecticut who came to California in 1847. He had previously been a lawyer and an officer of the New York Militia. In 1850 he became a printer in Sacramento before moving back east. He then returned to Los Angeles where he was the district attorney and later a county judge.

Manuel Dominguez, representing the District of Los Angeles, was a native of California. He was an *alcalde* (mayor) of both San Pedro and Los Angeles. In 1846 his rancho was occupied by Americans. In 1852 he served as a county supervisor before retiring to his rancho.

Alfred J. Ellis, representing the District of San Francisco, was a native of New York who came to California in 1847. He was a merchant who traveled back and forth between San Francisco and Honolulu, and also owned a boarding-house in San Francisco.

Stephen Clark Foster, representing the District of Los Angeles, was a native of Maine who came to California in 1847. He was a trader in northern Mexico, and then joined the Mormon Battalion to fight in the Mexican War. In 1854 he became the mayor of Los Angeles.

Edward C. Gilbert, representing the District of San Francisco, was a native of New York who came to California with a military unit recruited to fight in the Mexican War. He was the editor and owner of the *Alta California* newspaper. He served one term in the U.S. Congress. In 1852 he was killed in a duel with State Senator James W. Denver.

William M. Gwin, representing the District of San Francisco, was a native of Tennessee who came to California from Mississippi, where he had practiced medicine and served as a U.S. congressman. He was California's first U.S. senator. At the start of the Civil War, he was accused of disloyalty and was briefly jailed. After his release he moved to France.

Henry W. Halleck, representing the District of Monterey, was a native of New York who came to California as an army officer in 1847. He served as secretary of state to military governors Mason and Riley. His law firm became the largest in San Francisco and made him extremely wealthy. During the Civil War, he served as President Lincoln's chief of staff, and then became a general commanding the Department of the Pacific.

Julian Hanks, representing the District of San Jose, was a native of Connecticut who came to California in 1845 aboard the *Maria Teresa*. He was a farmer and active in San Jose politics.

Lansford W. Hastings, representing the District of Sacramento, was a native of Ohio who led an overland expedition to Oregon in 1842, and then came to California the next year. He returned east and published the *Emigrants' Guide*, urging settlers heading west to take a new route which went through the desert south of the Great Salt Lake. Its use led to the tragedy of the Donner Party. He worked as a lawyer and businessman, and at the end of his life moved to Brazil.

Henry Hill, representing the District of San Diego, was a native of Virginia who came to California in 1848 as a member of the U.S. Army.

Joseph Hobson, representing the District of San Francisco, was a native of Maryland who came to California in 1848 aboard the *Lady Adams*.

Capitol building 1849-51,
located at what is today the 100 block of South Market Street in San Jose.
Building was destroyed by fire in 1853.

John McHenry Hollingsworth, representing the District of San Joaquin, was a native of Maryland who came to California in 1847. He was previously a lieutenant in the New York Volunteers. In 1874, he moved to Washington, D.C.

Jacob D. Hoppe, representing the District of San Jose, was a native of Maryland who came to California in 1846. He was a landowner and editor of the *Californian*. He made a fortune in mining, but then lost it all by speculation. In 1853 he was killed by an explosion aboard the *Jenny Lind*.

James M. Jones, representing the District of San Joaquin, was a native of Kentucky who came to California in 1849. He was a lawyer, district judge, and an excellent linguist.

Thomas Oliver Larkin, representing the District of Monterey, was a native of Massachusetts who came to California by ship in 1832 to join his half-brother, John R. Cooper. His wife, Rachel Holmes, became the first American woman to live in California and his son, Thomas Larkin, Jr., became the first child of American parents to be born in California. He served as a U.S. consul from 1844-48. He owned a great deal of property and is credited with introducing the colonial style of architecture to Monterey.

Francis J. Lippett, representing the District of San Francisco, was a native of Rhode Island who came to California in 1847. He was a commander of the garrison at Santa Barbara. In 1848, he moved to San Francisco to practice law. He served in the U.S. Army from 1861-65 during the Civil War.

Benjamin S. Lippincott, representing the District of San Joaquin, was a native of New York who came to California in 1845. On his journey out, he was wounded during a skirmish. He was a trader and a gambler, and was a member of the first State Legislature.

M. M. McCarver, representing the District of Sacramento, was a native of Kentucky who came to California in 1848 from Oregon. He was a farmer and moved to Idaho in the 1850s.

John McDougal, representing the District of Sacramento, was a native of Ohio who came to California in 1849. He was a distinguished army officer who served in the Black Hawk and Mexican wars. He was elected California's first lieutenant governor, and then became governor upon the resignation of Peter Burnett.

Benjamin F. Moore, representing the District of San Joaquin, was a native of Florida who came to California in 1848. He was one of the earliest settlers at Sonora.

Myron Norton, representing the District of San Francisco, was a native of Vermont who came to California in 1848 aboard the *Huntress*. He was a lawyer who was very active in organizing the civil government in San Francisco. He served as a district judge and was an unsuccessful candidate for the Supreme Court.

Pacificus Ord, representing the District of Monterey, was a native of Maryland who came to California in 1849. He was a lawyer and U.S. attorney. His brother, Edward, was a famous military leader for whom Fort Ord is named.

Antonio María Pico, representing the District of San Jose, was a native of California born in Monterey. He was the grandson of Santiago de la Cruz Pico, who came to California in 1776 with the Anza expedition. He owned large amounts of land and was *alcalde* (mayor) of San Jose in 1835. In

1846 he purchased the Mission San Rafael estate. President Lincoln appointed him register of the U.S. Land Office in Los Angeles.

Rodman Price, representing the District of San Francisco, was a native of New York who came to California in 1845 as a member of the U.S. Navy. He left the military in 1847 and became a wealthy landowner. In 1850 he moved to New Jersey, where he later became state governor.

Hugo Reid, representing the District of Los Angeles, was a native of Scotland who came to California from Mexico in 1832. He was partners in a successful trading firm with Jacob Leese. He married an Indian woman from Mission San Gabriel and became owner of Rancho Santa Anita. In 1852 he wrote articles about California Indians for the *Los Angeles Star*.

Jacinto Rodriguez, representing the District of Monterey, was a native of California born in Monterey. He was a member of the military and worked for Mexican Governor Alvarado. In 1844 he was granted the Jacinto Rancho in Colusa.

Pedro Sansevaine, representing the District of San Jose, was a native of France who came to California in 1838. He mined along the Stanislaus River. Don Pedro Bar was named for him.

Robert B. Semple, representing the District of Sonoma, was a native of Kentucky who came to California with the Lansford Hastings party in 1845. He was a leader of the Bear Flag Revolt in 1846. Along with Walter Colton, he founded California's first newspaper, *The Californian*. He was also the founder of the town of Benicia.

William E. Shannon, representing the District of Sacramento, was a native of Ireland who came to California from New York in 1847. He was a lawyer and a partner in the trading firm of Shannon & Cady. He served briefly as a district judge, and died from cholera in 1850.

Winfield S. Sherwood, representing the District of Sacramento, was a native of New York and a member of the New York Legislature who came to California in 1849. He was a candidate for governor in California's first election, but ran second to Peter Burnett.

Jacob R. Snyder, representing the District of Sacramento, was a native of Pennsylvania who came to California in 1845 as part of the Swasey-Todd party. He was a surveyor and a major in the California Battalion. He was a State senator from 1852-53 and treasurer of the U.S. mint in San Francisco from 1853-60.

Abel Stearns, representing the District of Los Angeles, was a native of Massachusetts who came to California in 1829 after spending three years in Mexico. His marriage into the Bandini family made him the largest landowner and cattleman in southern California. He was a leader in the movements that overthrew Mexican governors Victoria and Micheltorena, and secretly worked with Thomas Larkin to obtain American control of California.

William M. Steuart, representing the District of San Francisco, was a native of Maryland who came to California in 1848. He was a major landowner, justice of the peace, and unsuccessful candidate in California's first election for governor.

John Augustus Sutter, representing the District of Sacramento, was a native of Switzerland who came to California in 1839 after spending five years in New York, Missouri, Oregon, and Hawaii. He was granted a large rancho at the junction of the Sacramento and American rivers. A large farm and fort were built on the property and used for military purposes and as a trading headquarters for American settlers. In 1848 gold was discovered on his property and the great gold rush began. His workers deserted him, his rancho was ruined and squatters took over his property. He moved to Pennsylvania and died a poor man.

Henry A. Tefft, representing the District of San Luis Obispo, was a native of New York who came to California in 1849. He was a lawyer and district judge.

Mariano Guadalupe Vallejo, representing the District of Sonoma, was a native of California born in Monterey. His military service under Mexico included command of northern California in the 1830s. He was granted several large ranchos, including the land at Sonoma where the Bear Flag Revolt happened. After joining the movement to make California part of the U.S., he served in the first State Legislature.

Thomas L. Vermeule, representing the District of San Joaquin, was a native of New Jersey who came to California from New York in 1847. He was a lawyer and newspaper writer.

Joel P. Walker, representing the District of Sonoma, was a native of Virginia who originally came to California from Oregon in 1841. He returned to Oregon in 1843 and worked as a cattleman. In 1848 he came back to California and purchased land in San Francisco. He was the first assessor of Napa County.

Oliver Meredith Wozencraft, representing the District of San Joaquin, was a native of Louisiana who came to California as a doctor in 1849. In 1850 he became a U. S. commissioner in charge of negotiating treaties with the local Indian tribes. Later, he became the first person to propose the idea of using the Colorado River to irrigate the Imperial Valley.

Capitol building 1852-53,
located in Vallejo; later destroyed by fire

5

The articles of California's first constitution

A constitution consists of multiple parts (or chapters) and each part is known as an *article*. Each article also consists of multiple parts; each part within an article is known as a *section*. At the very beginning of a constitution, before the first article, is a *preamble*, which briefly states the constitution's overall purpose.

PREAMBLE
We, the people of California, grateful to Almighty God for our freedom; in order to secure its blessings, do establish this Constitution:

California's first constitution (known as the Constitution of 1849) has 12 articles, which are summarized below.

ARTICLE I. DECLARATION OF RIGHTS
Basic rights guaranteed to all citizens.

Section 1. Inalienable Rights of Men
People by nature are free and have inalienable (can not be taken away) rights including enjoying life and liberty, acquiring property, and obtaining safety and happiness.

Section 2. Government For and By the People
All the power of government belongs to the people and the government is designed for their protection and benefit.

Section 3. Jury Trial
Anyone accused of a crime has the right to a trial by a jury.

Section 4. Freedom of Religion
Everyone has the freedom to practice their own religion as long as it does not interfere with the peace or safety of the State.

Section 5. Habeas Corpus

No person may be wrongfully imprisoned by the police; any person who is arrested must be charged with a crime or released.

Sections 6-7. Bail and Witnesses

Bail (the amount of money required to be paid by a person accused of a crime to allow him or her to be released from jail until the completion of the trial) may not be charged in excessive amounts. All persons have the right to bail unless they are charged with a capital crime. Witnesses may not be detained for unreasonable amounts of time.

Section 8. Criminal Trials--Rights of the Accused

Any person accused of a crime has certain rights, including the rights to appear in person, to have a lawyer present, and not to be charged twice for the same crime (double-jeopardy).

Section 9. Freedom of Speech

Each citizen has the right to speak, write, and publish his or her views on all subjects as long as they are responsible for any abuses of this right.

Section 10. Freedom of Assembling and Petitioning

People have the right to gather together for any purpose as well as the right to petition the government to address their concerns.

Section 11. Laws to be Uniform

All laws are to be applied to all people equally.

Section 12. Military Subordinate to Civil Power

The civil (elected) government shall have control over the military.

Section 13. Quartering of Soldiers

No individual shall be required to have a soldier live in his/her home in times of peace. In times of war, this may only be required if authorized by the Legislature.

Section 14. Representation According to Population

Each district (area) of the state will have the number of representatives in the Legislature based on its population.

Section 15. Imprisonment for Debt and Militia Fines Forbidden

No person shall be imprisoned for debt unless they have committed fraud. Also prevents imprisonment for failure to pay a militia (military) fine during times of peace.

Section 16. *Bills of Attainder* and *Ex Post Facto Laws*

Both *bills of attainder* and ex *post facto laws* are prohibited. A *bill of attainder* takes away a person's property or civil rights without a trial. An *ex post facto law* can make an act a crime even if it was committed before the law was passed.

Section 17. Rights of Foreigners

All foreign born persons who become legal residents of the State have the same rights as native born citizens.

Section 18. Slavery Prohibited

Slavery is prohibited. (Slavery was legal in many other states in 1849.)

Section 19. Unreasonable Search and Seizure

Persons or their property may not be searched without a warrant issued by the government upon probable cause to believe a crime has been committed.

Section 20. Treason

The acts that constitute treason are defined; the testimony of two witnesses is required in order to be convicted.

Section 21. Rights Retained by the People

The stating of these rights does not imply that these are the only rights that the people have.

ARTICLE II. RIGHT OF SUFFRAGE

The right of suffrage means the right to vote.

Section 1. Who May Vote, Who May Not

Right to vote granted to white males age 21 or older who have been residents of the State for at least six months and are either a citizen of the United States, or a citizen of Mexico who elected to become a citizen of the Untied States under a United States-Mexico peace treaty. Also authorizes the Legislature to decide if Indians (Native Californians) should have the right to vote.

Section 2. Privileges of Voters

Except in cases of treason or felony (a major crime), no person can be arrested on election day.

Section 3. Voters Not Obliged to Perform Military Duty on Election Day

No voter can be required to perform military duty on election day except in time of war.

Section 4. Residence of Voters

No one shall lose or gain residence status while serving in the United States government (in the military or civil government), nor while attending college.

Section 5. Person Not Entitled to Privileges of an Elector

Mentally ill persons are not entitled to vote. Persons who have been convicted of an infamous (notorious) crime are also not allowed to vote.

Section 6. Election to be by Ballot

All elections shall be by ballot.

ARTICLE III. DISTRIBUTION OF POWER

Sets up the executive, legislative, and judicial branches of government and prohibits any person from serving in more than one branch at the same time.

ARTICLE IV. LEGISLATIVE DEPARTMENT

The Senate and Assembly make up the two units of the Legislature. Sessions of the Legislature will be annual. Members of the Assembly will be elected for one-year terms and senators will be elected for two-year terms. The Assembly has the power to impeach the governor (and other state-wide officers) with the Senate to act as the jury (similar to the Federal government). The Legislature is prohibited from granting divorces, establishing a lottery, creating paper money and chartering banks. Legislators must be residents of their district for at least six months and residents of the State for at least one year.

ARTICLE V. EXECUTIVE DEPARTMENT

The governor is the supreme executive officer as well as commander-in-chief of the state militia. The term of office is for two years and a person must be a resident of the State for at least two years and be at least

25 years old in order to be eligible for the office. Other state-wide officers are lieutenant governor, comptroller, treasurer, attorney general, and surveyor general. If the governor dies or is removed from office, then the lieutenant governor will become governor. The governor has the power to pardon persons convicted of a crime and to call special sessions of the Legislature.

ARTICLE VI. JUDICIAL DEPARTMENT

The judicial power in the State will consist of a Supreme Court, District Courts, County Courts, and Justices of the Peace. The Supreme Court will consists of a Chief Justice and two Associate Justices. Supreme Court Justices will be elected and serve six-year terms. The Legislature will determine the number of judicial districts in the state and the number of Justices of the Peace to be elected in each city and township.

ARTICLE VII. MILITIA

The Legislature shall provide for organizing the militia and the governor will have the authority to call upon the militia to execute the laws of the State, to suppress uprisings, and to repel (stop) invasions.

ARTICLE VIII. STATE DEBTS

The Legislature is prohibited from creating a debt greater than $300,000 except in the case of war or other similar emergency. Additional debt can be created for a particular project if it is approved by the voters.

ARTICLE IX. EDUCATION

A Superintendent of Public Instruction will be elected and serve for a three-year term. The Legislature will provide for a system of common schools and ensure that all school districts meet designated standards. A State University will be established on land granted to the State of California by the Federal government.

ARTICLE X. MODE OF AMENDING AND REVISING THE CONSTITUTION

An amendment (change) to the constitution may be proposed by a member of the Assembly or the Senate. If a majority of both houses approve the amendment, then it is recorded in their journals until the next Legislature is elected. If the majority of both houses of the next Legislature approve the amendment, then it is voted on by the people of the State. If the majority of the people approve the amendment, then the constitution is changed.

If two-thirds of both houses of the Legislature believe the entire constitution should be changed or revised, then they can call for a constitutional convention. A vote will then be taken and if the majority of the people approve, a constitutional convention will be held and a new or revised constitution will be written.

ARTICLE XI. MISCELLANEOUS PROVISIONS

San Jose is designated as the State capital. Other provisions include the outlawing of duels for office-holders, the establishment of an oath of office for state-wide officials, the ability for husbands and wives to have separate property, and the requirement that all laws and official publications be written in both English and Spanish.

ARTICLE XII. BOUNDARY

The northern boundary is the 42nd degree of north latitude. The southern boundary is the boundary line established by treaty between the United States and Mexico. The western boundary is the Pacific Ocean. The eastern boundary follows the 120th degree of west longitude between the 39th and 42nd degrees of north latitude, then makes a straight south-easterly line until it meets the Colorado River at the 35th degree of north latitude.

6

The constitutional convention of 1878-79

Although minor changes can occur by the amendment process, in order for a major revision of the Constitution to take place, a new constitutional convention needs to be called. In order for this to take place, two-thirds of the members of the Legislature must request the convention and the majority of the voters then must approve it. This has happened only once in the nearly 150 years since California became a state.

The 1870's brought hard times to California. In 1873 the nation experienced a great business depression with the full impact of it reaching California in 1875. Additionally, in the winter of 1876-77 California experienced a terrible drought. There was not enough water to operate the mines or take care of the crops and livestock. The combination of the business depression and drought lead to a large number of people being unemployed.

Many people were frustrated and much of their anger was aimed at large corporations. The Central Pacific Railroad was the largest landowner and employer in the state, and charged unfair prices for their services and often times insisted that bribes be paid to them. The mines were owned by large corporations rather than individual diggers, and they did not treat their employees well. Many people felt that the Constitution of 1849 had given the Legislature too much power, and that the Legislature often acted in the best interest of the large corporations, rather than the best interest of the people.

The leader of the movement calling for a new constitutional convention was Dennis Kearney, a native of Ireland who came to San Francisco in 1868. He founded a new political party known as the Workingmen's party. In addition to opposing the large corporations and railroads, they were opposed to Chinese immigrants, arguing that the Chinese worked for lower wages and took jobs away from others. In 1876 the Legislature passed the act calling for a constitutional convention and it was approved by the voters in September 1877.

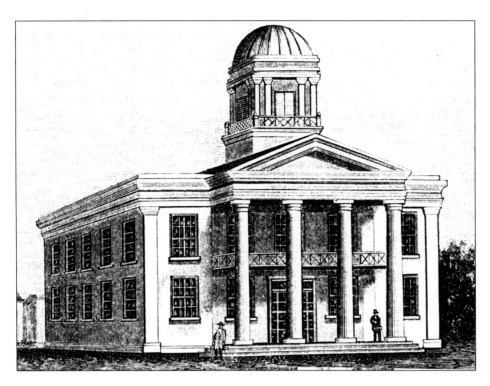

Sacramento's first courthouse at Seventh and I streets
used by the State legislature for the 1852 session and again in 1854

The convention was to be attended by 152 delegates. Three delegates were to be elected from each of the 40 senatorial districts, and 32 were to be elected statewide. The election was held on June 19, 1878. The Workingmen's party hoped to elect a majority of the delegates. They were only able, however, to elect 51 delegates (the rest were either Republicans, Democrats or independents). Although they did not have a majority, the Workingmen's party elected enough delegates to have a large amount of influence.

The majority of delegates were either lawyers, farmers, or merchants. Two delegates were natives of California and twenty were natives of foreign countries. The convention opened in Sacramento on September 28, 1878. J. P. Hoge was elected president of the Convention. The major features of the original constitution (the declaration of rights, the separation of powers, and the determination of who has the right to vote) were mostly left in tact. The delegates briefly discussed allowing women the right to vote, but then decided against it.

The major issues the delegates dealt with were corporate power, taxation and land reform, anti-Chinese racism, distrust of the Legislature, and the independent role of the California Constitution as it related to the U.S. Constitution. Many new sections were added limiting the power of corporations. A railroad commission was established and the commissioners (elected by the people) would be the ones to set the rates. New taxation methods were added that made corporations pay their fair share and discouraged the accumulation of large amounts of land. Small farmers received the same tax rights as large corporation farms. Chinese immigrants were specifically denied many rights and corporations were forbidden to hire Chinese employees. Many restrictions were imposed on the Legislature, and on people trying to influence individual legislators. Finally, the delegates emphasized the importance of the California Constitution and declared that the "Rights granted by this constitution are not dependent on those guaranteed by the United States Constitution."

After working for over five months, the delegates completed the new constitution on March 3, 1879. Twelve new articles had been added. Although fifteen delegates voted against approving the constitution, all of the delegates present agreed to sign it. The vote for approval by the people took place on May 7, 1879. Since corporations would lose much of their power, they argued heavily against it. The vote was close, but the new constitution was approved by a vote of 77,959 to 67,134.

This new constitution, known as the Constitution of 1879, has been amended many times, but is still in effect today.

Signers of the Constitution of 1879[1]

A. R. Andrews
James J. Ayers
Clitus Barbour
Edward Barry
James N. Barton
C. J. Beerstecher
Isaac S. Belcher
Peter Bell
Marion Biggs
E. T. Blackmer
Joseph C. Brown

Saml. B. Burt
Josiah Boucher
James Caples
Aug. H. Chapman
J. M. Charles
John D. Condon
C. W. Cross
Hamlet Davis
Jas. E. Dean
P. T. Dowling
Luke D. Doyle

[1] Only 139 members were present for the signing.

Capitol building 1853-54, located at First and G streets in Benicia

Capitol building 1855-69, at 7th and I streets in Sacramento

W. L. Dudley
Jonathan M. Dudley
Presley Dunlap
John Eagon
Thomas H. Estey
Henry Edgerton
M. M. Estee
Edward Evey
J. A. Filcher
Simon J. Farrell
Abraham Clark Freeman
Jacob Richard Freud
J. B. Garvey
B. B. Glascock
Joseph G. Gorman
W. P. Grace
William J. Graves
V. A. Gregg
Jno. S. Hager
John B. Hall
Thomas Harrison
Joel A. Harvey
T. D. Heiskell
Conrad Herold
D. W. Herrington
S. G. Hilborn
J. R. W. Hitchcock
J. E. Hale
J. P. Hoge
Volney E. Howard
Sam. A. Holmes
W. J. Howard
Wm. Proctor Hughey
W. F. Huestis
G. W. Hunter
Daniel Inman
George A. Johnson
L. F. Jones
Peter J. Joce
J. M. Kelley
James H. Keyes

John J. Kenny
C. R. Kleine
T. H. Laine
Henry Larkin
R. M. Lampson
R. Lavigne
H. M. Laure
David Lewis
J. F. Lindow
Jno. Mansfield
Edward Martin
J. West Martin
Rush McComas
John G. McCallum
Thomas McConnell
John McCoy
Thomas B. McFarland
Hiram Mills
Wm. S. Moffatt
John Fleming McNutt
W. W. Moreland
L. D. Morse
James E. Murphy
Edmund Nason
Thorwald Klaudius Nelson
Henry Neunaber
Chs. C. O'Donnell
George Ohleyer
James O'Sullivan
James Martin Porter
William H. Prouty
M. R. C. Pulliam
Chas. F. Reed
Patrick Reddy
Jno. M. Rhodes
Jas. S. Reynolds
Horace C. Rolfe
Chas. S. Ringgold
James McM. Shafter
Geo. W. Schell
J. Schomp

Rufus Shoemaker
Benj. Shurtleff
E. O. Smith
Geo. Venable Smith
H. W. Smith
John C. Stedman
E. P. Soule
D. C. Stevenson
George Steele
Chas. V. Stuart
W. J. Sweasey
Charles Swenson
R. S. Swing
D. S. Terry
S. B. Thompson
F. O. Townsend
W. J. Tinnin
Daniel Tuttle

P. B. Tully
H. K. Turner
A. P. Vacquerel
Walter Van Dyke
Wm. Van Voorhies
Hugh Walker
Jno. Walker
Byron Waters
Joseph R. Weller
J. V. Webster
John P. West
Patrick M. Wellin
John T. Wickes
Wm. F. White
H. C. Wilson
Jos. W. Winans
N. G. Wyatt

Capitol building, 1869 to present, located on L Street in Sacramento

7

The articles of California's current constitution

California's current constitution (known as the Constitution of 1879) has been amended hundreds of times since it was written in 1879. In fact, it is now the longest constitution of all fifty states. The constitution became much easier to amend in 1911 when the initiative process was first allowed. This meant that the voters could directly propose an amendment without first going through the Legislature.

PREAMBLE
We, the people of California, grateful to Almighty God for our freedom; in order to secure and perpetuate its blessings, do establish this Constitution:

California's current constitution (including all its amendments) now has twenty articles, which are summarized below. (The numbering system goes up to 34 because 14 articles have been repealed [removed].)

ARTICLE I. DECLARATION OF RIGHTS
Basic rights guaranteed to all citizens.

Section 1. Inalienable Rights of Men
People by nature are free and have inalienable (can not be taken away) rights including enjoying life and liberty, acquiring property, and obtaining safety and happiness.

Section 2. Freedom of Speech and of the Press
Each citizen has the right to speak, write, and publish his or her views on all subjects as long as they are responsible for any abuses of this right. News reporters are protected from having to reveal their sources of information.

Section 3. Freedom of Assembling and Petitioning
People have the right to gather together for any purpose as well as the right to petition the government to address their concerns.

Section 4. Freedom of Religion

Everyone has the freedom to practice their own religion as long as it does not interfere with the peace or safety of the State. No person may be prohibited from serving on a jury or as a witness because of his or her religious beliefs.

Section 5. Military

The civil (elected) government shall have control over the military. A standing army may not be maintained in peacetime. No individual shall be required to have a soldier live in his/her home in times of peace. In times of war, this may only be required if authorized by the Legislature.

Section 6. Slavery Prohibited

Slavery is prohibited. Involuntary servitude is only allowed as punishment for crimes.

Section 7. Due Process of Law and School Bussing

Each citizen is to be treated equally and all laws are to be applied the same to all people. State courts may not order school bussing to achieve desegration of schools, even if the reason the schools were segregated was as a result of individuals not receiving due process.

Section 8. Discrimination in Employment

A person may not be disqualified in employment based on sex, race, creed, color, or national or ethnic origin.

Section 9. *Bills of Attainder* and *Ex Post Facto Laws*

Both *bills of attainder* and ex *post facto laws* are prohibited. A *bill of attainder* takes away a person's property or civil rights without a trial. An *ex post facto law* can make an act a crime even if it was committed before the law was passed.

Section 10. Witness Detention and Imprisonment for Debt

No witness may be unreasonably detained and no person may be imprisoned for a civil debt or for a militia fine during peacetime.

Section 11. Habeas Corpus

No person may be wrongfully imprisoned by the police; any person who is arrested must be charged with a crime or released.

Sections 12. Bail

Bail (the amount of money required to be paid by a person accused of a crime to allow him or her to be released from jail until the completion of the trial) may not be charged in excessive amounts. All persons have the right to bail unless they are charged with a capital or other serious crime.

Section 13. Unreasonable Search and Seizure

Persons or their property may not be searched without a warrant issued by the government upon probable cause to believe a crime has been committed.

Sections 14-15. Criminal Trials--Rights of the Accused

Any person accused of a crime has certain rights, including the rights to appear in person, to have a lawyer present, and not to be charged twice for the same crime (double-jeopardy). Persons who do not understand English are to be provided with an interpreter.

Section 16. Jury Trial

Anyone accused of a crime has the right to a trial by a jury. Also sets the number of jurors for varying types of trials.

Section 17. Cruel or Unusual Punishment

Cruel or unusual punishment and excessive fines are not allowed.

Section 18. Treason

The acts that constitute treason are defined; the testimony of two witnesses is required in order to be convicted.

Section 19. Eminent Domain

Private property may be taken from individuals when needed for a public purpose and when the property owner is fairly compensated.

Section 20. Rights of Noncitizens

Noncitizens have the same property rights as citizens.

Section 21. Separate Property of Husband and Wife

Property owned before marriage, or acquired during marriage by gift of inheritance, is separate property.

Section 22. No Property Qualification for Electors

Right to vote or run for office does not require the owning of property.

Section 23. Grand Juries

At least one grand jury shall be called each year in each county.

Section 24. Independence of the California Constitution

Rights guaranteed by the California Constitution are not dependent on rights guaranteed by the U.S. Constitution.

Section 25. Right to Fish

People shall have the right to fish upon all public lands unless they are set aside for fish hatcheries. No land should be sold by the State without reserving the right for the people to fish upon it. The Legislature may define the season when specific species of fish may be taken.

Section 26. Constitution Mandatory

Provisions in the Constitution are mandatory rather than just suggestions.

Section 27. Death Penalty

The death penalty is not considered to be cruel or unusual punishment.

Section 28. Victims Bill of Rights

Rights given to victims of crimes are outlined, including the right to restitution (repayment). Students are guaranteed the right to safe schools.

Section 29. Speedy and Public Trial

Persons accused of a crime have the right to a speedy and public trial.

Section 30. Hearsay Evidence

Hearsay evidence (evidence not directly seen by the witness) is allowed in preliminary hearings. Also allows criminal trials to be combined.

Section 31. Prohibition Against Preferential Treatment

No person or group shall be granted preferential treatment in public employment or education based on race, sex, color, ethnicity, or national origin.

ARTICLE II. VOTING, INITIATIVE, REFERENDUM AND RECALL

Section 1. Purpose of Government
All power is with the people and the purpose of government is for the protection, security and benefit of the people.

Section 2. Right to Vote
All United States citizens age 18 or older who are residents of the state may vote.

Section 3. Residence, Registration and Free Elections
The Legislature shall define "residence" and provide for registration and free elections.

Section 4. Disqualification of Voters
Persons who are mentally incompetent are ineligible to vote. Persons who are imprisoned or on parole for conviction of a felony are also ineligible to vote.

Section 5. Primary Elections for Partisan Offices and Open Presidential Primary
Primary elections will be held for partisan offices (those where candidates run as a member of a political party). The presidential primary ballot will include all recognized by the Secretary of State to be legitimate candidates.

Section 6. Nonpartisan Offices
All judicial, school, county and city offices shall be nonpartisan (candidates do not run as members of a political party). No political party may endorse a candidate for a nonpartisan office.

Section 7. Secret Voting
All elections shall be by secret ballot.

Section 8. Initiative
An initiative allows voters to propose statues (laws) and amendments to the constitution and to then approve or reject them. An initiative measure for a statute will be placed on the ballot if signatures are gathered by five percent of the number of voters in the previous gubernatorial (for governor) election. An initiative measure for a

consitutional amendment will be placed on the ballot if signatures are gathered by eight percent of the number of voters in the previous gubernatorial election. An initiative measure may not cover more than one subject.

Section 9. Referendum

A referendum allows the voters to propose or reject statues (laws) already passed by the Legislature. A referendum measure will be placed on the ballot if signatures are gathered by five percent of the number of voters in the previous gubernatorial election.

Sections 10-12. Initiative and Referendum

Miscellaneous items dealing with initiatives and referenda including the right for local initiatives and referenda and the prohibition of individual . persons being names in initiatives and referenda.

Sections 13-19. Recall

A recall allows the voters to remove an elected official from office. A recall measure for a statewide office holder will be placed on the ballot if signatures are gathered by twelve percent of the number of voters in the previous election for the office holder being recalled. Additionally, signatures must be gathered by at least one percent of the voters in at least five different counties. Non-statewide office holders require signatures be gathered by twenty percent of the voters in the previous election for the non-statewide office holder being recalled. Recall of local office holders is also allowed.

Section 20. Commencement of Term of Office

The term of office for statewide office holders begins on the first Monday after the January 1st following the election. The length of term of office is decided by the Legislature.

ARTICLE III. STATE OF CALIFORNIA

Provides for the distribution of power and sets up the executive, legislative, and judicial branches of government, as well as prohibits any person from serving in more than one branch at the same time. Makes Sacramento the state capital and English the official state language.

ARTICLE IV. LEGISLATIVE

The Senate and Assembly make up the two units of the Legislature. The Senate will consist of 40 members and the Assembly will consist of 80 members. Sessions of the Legislature will be begin the first Monday in December in even-numbered years and adjourn (end) by November 30 of the following odd-numbered year. Members of the Assembly will be elected for two-year terms and senators will be elected for four-year terms. No senator may serve more than two terms and no member of the Assembly may serve more than three terms. The Assembly has the power to impeach the governor (and other statewide officers) with the Senate to act as the jury (similar to the Federal government). Although the Legislature is prohibited from establishing a lottery, the California State Lottery is created by the Constitution.

ARTICLE V. EXECUTIVE

The governor is the supreme executive officer as well as commander-in-chief of the state militia. The term of office is for four years and a person must be a resident of the State for at least five years in order to be eligible for the office. No governor may serve more than two terms. Other state-wide officers are lieutenant governor, comptroller, treasurer, attorney general, and secretary of state. If the governor dies or is removed from office, then the lieutenant governor will become governor. The governor has the power to pardon persons convicted of a crime unless they have been convicted twice of a felony. In that case he or she must first receive the recommendation of the Supreme Court. The governor may call special sessions of the Legislature for specific purposes.

ARTICLE VI. JUDICIAL

The judicial power in the State will consist of a Supreme Court, Court of Appeal, Superior Courts (counties) and Municipal Courts (cities). The Supreme Court will consist of a Chief Justice and six Associate Justices. Supreme Court Justices and judges of the Court of Appeal are appointed by the governor. After their appointment, they must be approved by the voters in order to serve. Supreme Court Justices are appointed for twelve-year terms and Court of Appeal judges are appointed for six year-terms. Several commissions are established to monitor the performance of the members of the judiciary.

ARTICLE VII. PUBLIC OFFICERS AND EMPLOYEES

Establishes the structure of the civil service system. All state employees are to be selected on the basis of merit (their qualifications for the job).

ARTICLE VIII has been repealed

ARTICLE IX. EDUCATION

A Superintendent of Public Instruction will be elected and serve for a four-year term. A State Board of Education will be established. Each county will elect or appoint a county Superintendent of Schools. The Legislature will provide for a system of common schools and ensure that all school districts meet designated standards. No state money will be given to support any sectarian (religious) school. The University of California is established and administered by a Board of Regents.

ARTICLE X. WATER

Establishes rules and regulations dealing with all of California's water resources. Water has always played a vital role in the state.

ARTICLE XI. LOCAL GOVERNMENT

Establishes counties as the main legal subdivisions of the state, as well as establishes basic rules for county government. Allows for cities and towns to be established within a county.

ARTICLE XII. PUBLIC UTILITIES

Creates the Public Utilities Commission to regulate utilities such as electricity or telephone service.

ARTICLE XIII. TAXATION

Creates boards of equalization to make sure taxation is equal across the state. Allows for state income and sales tax. Requires that special local taxes must be approved by at least two-thirds of the voters.

ARTICLE XIV. LABOR RELATIONS

Provides for a minimum wage and the establishment of a worker's compensation system. Sets working conditions for prison inmates.

ARTICLE XV. USURY

Sets the maximum amount that can be charged for interest on loans at seven percent (with many exceptions making this article practically irrelevant).

ARTICLE XVI. PUBLIC FINANCE

The Legislature is prohibited from creating a debt greater than $300,000 except in the case of war or other similar emergency. Additional debt can be created for a particular project if it is approved by two-thirds of the Legislature and a majority of the voters. Also regulates public financing of local governments.

ARTICLE XVII has been repealed

ARTICLE XVIII. AMENDING AND REVISING THE CONSTITUTION

An amendment (change) to the constitution may be proposed by a member of the Assembly or the Senate. If two-thirds of both houses approve the amendment, then it is voted on by the people of the State. If the majority of the people approve the amendment, then the constitution is changed. An amendment may also be made by voter initiative. This means that the proposal for the amendment can come directly from the voters, rather than having to originate in the Legislature.

If two-thirds of both houses of the Legislature believe the entire constitution should be changed or revised, then they can call for a constitutional convention. A vote will then be taken and if the majority of the people approve, then a constitutional convention will be held and a new or revised constitution will be written.

ARTICLE XIX. MOTOR VEHICLE REVENUES

Requires that all revenues (money) from the gasoline tax be spent on either highway-related projects or on public transportation projects.

ARTICLE XX. MISCELLANEOUS SUBJECTS

Contains a variety of small, miscellaneous items.

ARTICLE XXI. REAPPORTIONMENT OF SENATE, ASSEMBLY, CONGRESSIONAL, AND BOARD OF EQUALIZATION DISTRICTS

Sets rules for reapportioning (changing boundaries) of districts after each national census.

ARTICLES XXII-XXVIII have been repealed

ARTICLES XXIX-XXXIII were never established

ARTICLE XXXIV. PUBLIC HOUSING PROJECT LAW

Requires voter approval for the state to construct any public housing projects.

Bibliography

California Firsts. Rockwell Dennis Hunt, Fearon, 1957.

"California Legal History," *Law Library Journal, v. 90:3, p447-80,* Myra K. Saunders, Summer 1998.

California Pioneer Register and Index, 1542-1848. Hubert Howe Bancroft, Regional Publishing, 1964.

The California State Constitution (Internet site) http://www.leginfo.ca.gov/const.html, 1999.

The California State Constitution: A Reference Guide. Joseph R. Grodin, et. al., Greenwood Press, 1993.

A Companion to California. James D. Hart, University of California Press, 1987.

Constitution of the State of California. California Legislature, 1931. (contains the original constitution of 1849)

The Constitution of the United States of America and the Constitution of the State of California. California Legislature Assembly, 1997-98.

Constitution Revision: History and Perspective. California Constitution Revision Commission, Forum on Government Reform, 1996.

Debates and Proceedings of the Constitutional Convention of the State of California, Convened at the City of Sacramento, Saturday, September 28, 1878. State Office, 1880-81.

The Genesis of California's First Constitution (1846-49). Rockwell Dennis Hunt, Johnson Reprint, 1973.

History of California. Hubert Howe Bancroft, The History Company, 1884-90.

A History of the California Constitution. John M. Peirce, California Legislature, 1931.

The Original Constitution of the State of California, 1849: the Engrossed Copy with the Official Spanish Translation. Telefact Foundation, 1965.

Report of the Debates in the Convention of California on the Formation of the State Constitution, in September and October, 1849. J. Ross Browne, Towers, 1850.

Statutes of California Passed at the Twenty-Third Session of the Legislature. State Office, 1880. (Contains the original constitution of 1879.)

The Story of California's Constitution and Laws. Anne B. Fisher, Pacific Books, 1953.

The World Book Encyclopedia. World Book, 1999.

Toucan Valley Publications, Inc.

ISBN 1-884925-97-9

90000>

BUILT

ON COAL

A history of Beverly, Edmonton's working class town

by Lawrence Herzog

Beverly Community Development Society
4004 118 Avenue
Edmonton, Alberta
T5W 1A1
(780) 477 6333

Canadian Cataloguing in Publication Data

Herzog, Lawrence
  Built on Coal: a history of Beverly, Edmonton's working class town

Includes Index
ISBN 0-9687421-0-6

 1. Beverly (Edmonton, Alta.)--History. 2. Edmonton (Alta.)--History. I. Beverly
Community Development Society. II. Title.

FC3696.52.H478 2000   971.23'34   C00-900865-9
F1079.5.E3H47 2000

Editor: Shirley Lowe
Graphic Design and Layout: Liz Bolduc Design
Printing: Jasper Printing, Edmonton.

Production of this book made possible through the generous support of the
Alberta Historical Resources Foundation, Real Estate Weekly and the Klondike
City Optimist Club.

Cover:

Beverly coal trucks in front of the Beverly Mine Tipple, 1937.
Photo by Hubert Hollingworth
City of Edmonton Archives, EA-160-218

Throughout the book, photos by the author unless otherwise noted.